It's A Good Thing There Are Insects

By Allan Fowler

Images supplied by VALAN Photos
and Jeffrey L. Rotman

Consultants:
Robert L. Hillerich, Ph.D., Bowling Green
State University, Bowling Green, Ohio

Mary Nalbandian, Director of Science,
Chicago Public Schools, Chicago, Illinois

SCHOLASTIC INC.

New York Toronto London Auckland Sydney
Mexico City New Delhi Hong Kong Buenos Aires

ISBN 0-516-44905-2

15 16 17 18 19 20 R   8/0

Printed in China. 62

First Scholastic printing, December 2001

Series cover and interior design by Sara Shelton

Sometimes we call them bugs. But their real name is insects.

All insects have six legs
like a grasshopper.

Most insects, like flies, have wings.

Some insects live in trees
like cicadas,

and some live in water
like water beetles.

Some insects, including most ants, make their home in the ground.

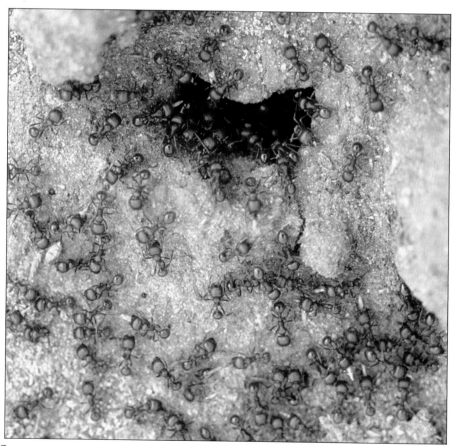

They have their own little
"town," where each ant
does its own kind of work.

A caterpillar forms a shell, called a chrysalis, around itself.

In the chrysalis, the
caterpillar changes into
a butterfly.

This home for bees is called a hive.

Some insects are harmful to people.

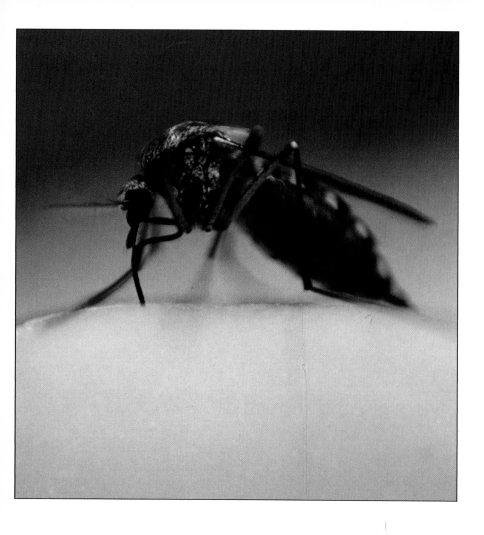

Mosquitoes can bite you.

Wasps can sting you.

Locusts can eat a farmer's crops.

But insects are helpful
to us in many ways.

We get silk from the
cocoon of a silkworm.

We get honey from
bees.

As bees fly from flower
to flower, they carry
pollen to help the flowers
grow.

Some insects are pretty
like this monarch butterfly.

Insects serve as food too.
Many animals and birds
and fish and reptiles live
by eating insects.

23

But they leave the walking
stick alone. They think
it's a twig!

Some insects glow in the dark like a firefly or a lightning bug.

Some insects make sounds
like a cricket.

So the next time you
see a beetle

or a lady bug,

remember—it's a good thing there are insects!

Words You Know

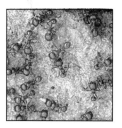

ants

bees
beehive

monarch
butterfly

chrysalis

cicada

cricket

fly

grasshopper

lady bug

lightning bug

locust

mosquito

silkworm cocoon

walking stick

wasp

water beetle

Index

About the Author

Allan Fowler is a free-lance writer with a background in advertising. Born in New York, he lives in Chicago now and enjoys traveling.

Photo Credits

Valan— © Herman H. Giethoorn, Cover, 4, 21, 26, 30 (top right, center right, bottom center); © Val & Alan Wilkinson, 5, 22, 24, 25, 30 (bottom left), 31 (center center & top left); © V. Whelan, 6, 28, 30 (center center & bottom right); © A. J. Bond, 7, 31 (bottom); © Kennon Cooke, 8, 30 (top left); © Dennis W. Schmidt, 9; © Pam Hickman, 10, 30 (center left); J. R. Page, 11, 14, 31 (top right); © S. J. Krasemann, 12, 16, 30 (top center), 31 (top center); © Harold V. Green, 15, 20, 31 (center right); © J. A. Wilkinson, 18, 31 (center left); © Michel Bourque, 19; © Jeff Foott, 23; © John Fowler, 27

COVER: Monarch butterfly